X

PUFFIN BOOKS

D0269122

THE PUFFIN BOOK OF CHRISTMAS POEMS

This delightful seasonal anthology for children
of all ages contains nearly 100 poems, mostly
contemporary but with the addition of some older
favourite and traditional pieces. The collection not
only includes such magical experiences as winter
sports, carol singing, Christmas Eve, opening
presents and the Nativity, but also covers
entertainment, creatures of the cold and spooky
winter tales. In other words, a Christmas stocking
packed with surprises and good things.

Wes Magee is head teacher in a primary school and
is also an author, editor and lecturer, frequently
visiting schools to give poetry workshops for
children. He lives near York with his wife and two
children.

THE
PUFFIN BOOK
OF
CHRISTMAS POEMS

Compiled by Wes Magee

Illustrated by Jill Bennett

PUFFIN BOOKS

PUFFIN BOOKS

Published by the Penguin Group
Penguin Books Ltd, 27 Wrights Lane, London W8 5TZ, England
Viking Penguin, a division of Penguin Books USA Inc.
375 Hudson Street, New York, New York 10014, USA
Penguin Books Australia Ltd, Ringwood, Victoria, Australia
Penguin Books Canada Ltd, 2801 John Street, Markham, Ontario, Canada L3R 1B4
Penguin Books (NZ) Ltd, 182–190 Wairau Road, Auckland 10, New Zealand

Penguin Books Ltd, Registered Offices: Harmondsworth, Middlesex, England

First published as *A Christmas Stocking* by Cassell Educational Limited 1988
Published in Puffin Books 1990
10 9 8 7 6 5 4 3 2 1

The Acknowledgements on pages 138–40 constitute an extension of this copyright page

Filmset in Melior
Printed and bound in Great Britain by
Cox & Wyman Ltd, Reading, Berks.

Carols drift across the night
Holly gleams by candlelight
Roaring fire, a spooky tale
Ice and snow and wind and hail
Santa seen in High Street store
Television . . . more and *more*
Mince pies, turkey, glass of wine
Acting your own pantomime
Socks hung up. It's Christmas time!

Wes Magee

Contents

In the Week when Christmas Comes

Feed the Birds

Sports . . . and Entertainments

Winter Weather

The Night before Christmas

Merry Christmas!

A New Star

Winter Tales

Snow on Snow

Snow at School

Vera Wyse

A whisper stirred the stale air
In the sleepy classroom.
Heads turned, eyes brightened as
From the overburdened sky
one flake fell.
Faster faster feathery winter
Covered the playground
With a blanket of delight.
'It's snowing, pass it on,' rippled round the room.
Pens scurried, backs straightened,
Chairs scraped under desks.
Coats shrugged on shoulders, out, out
To be the first to plant a footstep,
Make a mark that wouldn't matter tomorrow
But was vital today!

Winter Morning

Clive Sansom

No one has ever been here before,
Never before!
Snow is stretching, pure and white,
From the back door
To where that elm tree by the coppice-fence
Stands black and bare,
With never a footprint, never a clawprint
Anywhere!
Only the clean, white page of snow
In front of me,
With the long shadow of a single tree
For company.

When all the World is full of Snow

I never know
just where to go,
when all the world
is full of snow.

I do not want
to make a track,
not even
to the shed and back.

I only want
to watch and wait,
while snow moths settle
on the gate,

and swarming frost flakes
fill the trees
with billions
of albino bees.

I want to watch
the snow swarms thin,
till all my bees
have settled in,

and on the ice
the boulders ride,
like sleeping snow geese
on the tide.

I only want
myself to be
as silent as
a winter tree,

to hear the swirling
stillness grow,
when all the world
is full of snow.

N M Bodecker

Snow and Snow

Ted Hughes

Snow is sometimes a she, a soft one.
   Her kiss on your cheek, her finger on your sleeve
In early December, on a warm evening,
     And you turn to meet her, saying 'It's snowing!'
       But it is not. And nobody's there.
       Empty and calm is the air.

Sometimes the snow is a he, a sly one.
   Weakly he signs the dry stone with a damp spot.
Waifish he floats and touches the pond and is not.
     Treacherous-beggarly he falters, and taps at the
          window.
       A little longer he clings to the grass-blade tip
       Getting his grip.

Then how she leans, how furry foxwrap she nestles
     The sky with her warm, and the earth with her
          softness.
How her lit crowding fairytales sink through the space-
          silence
     To build her palace, till it twinkles in starlight —
       Too frail for a foot
       Or a crumb of soot.

Then how his muffled armies move in all night
    And we wake and every road is blockaded
Every hill taken and every farm occupied
    And the white glare of his tents is on the ceiling.
        And all that dull blue day and on into the gloaming
        We have to watch more coming.

Then everything in the rubbish-heaped world
    Is a bridesmaid at her miracle.
Dunghills and crumbly dark old barns are bowed in the
            chapel of her sparkle,
    The gruesome boggy cellars of the wood
        Are a wedding of lace
        Now taking place.

White Fields

James Stephens

In the winter time we go
Walking in the fields of snow;

Where there is no grass at all;
Where the top of every wall,

Every fence and every tree
Is as white as white can be.

Pointing out the way we came —
Every one of them the same —

All across the fields there be
Prints in silver filigree;

And our mothers always know,
By the footprints in the snow,

Where it is the children go.

Footsteps in the Snow

Anne English

Overnight the snow fell, covering the street
With a smooth white blanket.
Look at it now, trampled by feet
In boots and shoes and wellingtons.
There are giant steps and tiny ones,
Smooth steps and wavy ones,
Straight steps and crooked ones,

    And

         these

    are

        MINE.

In the bleak mid-winter

Christina Rossetti

In the bleak mid-winter
  Frosty wind made moan,
Earth stood hard as iron,
  Water like a stone.
Snow had fallen
  Snow on snow
  Snow on snow
In the bleak mid-winter
  Long, long ago.

Carolling around the Estate

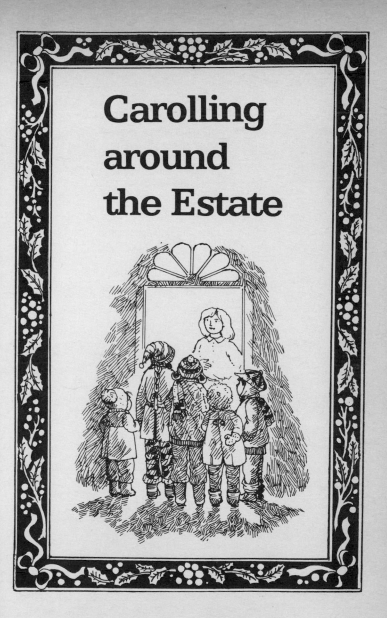

The Children's Carol

Eleanor Farjeon

Here we come again, again, and here we come again,
Christmas is a single pearl swinging on a chain,
Christmas is a single flower in a barren wood,
Christmas is a single sail on the salty flood,
Christmas is a single star in the empty sky,
Christmas is a single song sung for charity.
Here we come again, again, to sing to you again,
Give a single penny that we may not sing in vain.

Carolling around the Estate

Wes Magee

The six of us met at Alan's house
    and Jane brought a carol sheet
that she'd got free from the butcher's shop
    when she bought the Sunday meat.

Jeremy had a new lantern light
    made by his Uncle Ted,
and Jim had 'borrowed' his dad's new torch
    which flashed white, green and red.

Our first call was at Stew Foster's place
    where we sang 'Three Kings' real well
but his mother couldn't stand the row
    and she really gave us hell!

We drifted on from door to door
    singing carols by lantern light.
Jane's lips were purple with the cold;
    my fingers were turning white.

Around nine we reached the chippie shop
    where we ordered pies and peas,
and with hot grease running down our hands
    we started to defreeze.

I reached home tired out, but my mum said,
    'Your cousin Anne's been here.
She's carolling tomorrow night
    and I said you'd go, my dear.'

Christmas is Coming!

Anon

Christmas is coming,
    The geese are getting fat,
Please put a penny
    In the old man's hat.
If you haven't got a penny,
    A ha'penny will do.
If you haven't got a ha'penny
    Then God bless you!

We wish you a Merry Christmas

Anon

We wish you a Merry Christmas.
We wish you a Merry Christmas.
We wish you a Merry Christmas
And a Happy New Year.

Good tidings we bring
For you and your kin.
We wish you a Merry Christmas
And a Happy New Year.

Now bring us some figgie pudding.
Now bring us some figgie pudding.
Now bring us some figgie pudding.
Now bring some right here!

We won't go until we've got some.
We won't go until we've got some.
We won't go until we've got some.
So bring some right here!

We wish you a Merry Christmas.
We wish you a Merry Christmas.
We wish you a Merry Christmas
And a Happy New Year.

The Wicked Singers

And have you been out carol singing,
Collecting for the Old Folk's Dinner?

Oh yes indeed, oh yes indeed.

And did you sing all the Christmas numbers,
Every one a winner?

Oh yes indeed, oh yes indeed.

Good King Wenceslas, and Hark
The Herald Angels Sing?

Oh yes indeed, oh yes indeed.

And did you sing them loud and clear
And make the night sky ring?

      Oh yes indeed, oh yes indeed.

And did you count up all the money?
Was it quite a lot?

      Oh yes indeed, oh yes indeed.

And did you give it all to the Vicar,
Everything you'd got?

      Certainly not, certainly not.

                Kit Wright

The Carol Singers

Margaret Rhodes

Last night the carol singers came
    When I had gone to bed,
Upon the crisp white path outside
    I heard them softly tread.

I sat upright to listen, for
    I knew they came to tell,
Of all the things that happened on
    The very first Noel.

Upon my ceiling flickering
    I saw their lantern glow,
And then they sang their carols sweet
    Of Christmas long ago.

Creatures
of the Cold

Furry Bear

A A Milne

If I were a bear
    And a big bear too,
I shouldn't much care
    If it froze or snew;
I wouldn't much mind
    If it snowed or friz —
I'd be all fur-lined
    With a coat like his!

For I'd have fur boots and a brown fur wrap,
And brown fur knickers and a big fur cap.
I'd have a fur muffle-ruff to cover my jaws,
And brown fur mittens on my big brown paws.
With a big brown furry-down up on my head,
I'd sleep all winter in a big fur bed.

Sheep in Winter

John Clare

The sheep get up and make their many tracks
And bear a load of snow upon their backs,
And gnaw the frozen turnip to the ground
With sharp quick bite, and then go nosing round
The boy that pecks the turnips all the day
And knocks his hands to keep the cold away
And laps his legs in straw to keep them warm
And hides behind the hedges from the storm.
The sheep, as tame as dogs, go where he goes
And try to shake their fleeces from the snows,
Then leave their frozen meal and wander round
The stubble stack that stands beside the ground,
And lie all night and face the drizzling storm
And shun the hovel where they might be warm.

Small, smaller

Russell Hoban

I thought that I knew all there was to know
Of being small, until I saw once, black against the snow,
A shrew, trapped in my footprint, jump and fall
And jump again and fall, the hole too deep, the walls too
        tall.

From the winter wind

Michael Rosen

From the winter wind
a cold fly
came to our window
where we had frozen our noses
and warmed his feet on the glass.

On a Night of Snow

Elizabeth Coatsworth

Cat, if you go outdoors you must walk in the snow.
You will come back with little white shoes on your feet,
Little white slippers of snow that have heels of sleet.
Stay by the fire, my Cat. Lie still, do not go.
See how the flames are leaping and hissing low,
I will bring you a saucer of milk like a marguerite,
So white and so smooth, so spherical and so sweet—
Stay with me, Cat. Outdoors the wild winds blow.

Outdoors the wild winds blow, Mistress, and dark is the
          night.
Strange voices cry in the trees, intoning strange lore;
And more than cats move, lit by our eyes' green light,
On silent feet where the meadow grasses hang hoar—
Mistress, there are portents abroad of magic and might,
And things that are yet to be done. Open the door!

The Fallow Deer at the Lonely House

One without looks in tonight
  Through the curtain-chink
From the sheet of glistening white;
One without looks in tonight
  As we sit and think
  By the fender-brink.

We do not discern those eyes
    Watching in the snow;
Lit by lamps of rosy dyes
We do not discern those eyes
    Wondering, aglow,
    Fourfooted, tiptoe.

Thomas Hardy

Amulet

Ted Hughes

Inside the wolf's fang, the mountain of heather.
Inside the mountain of heather, the wolf's fur.
Inside the wolf's fur, the ragged forest.
Inside the ragged forest, the wolf's foot.
Inside the wolf's foot, the stony horizon.
Inside the stony horizon, the wolf's tongue.
Inside the wolf's tongue, the doe's tears.
Inside the doe's tears, the frozen swamp.
Inside the frozen swamp, the wolf's blood.
Inside the wolf's blood, the snow wind.
Inside the snow wind, the wolf's eye.
Inside the wolf's eye, the North star.
Inside the North star, the wolf's fang.

In the Week when Christmas Comes

Time to go Christmas Shopping

Jane Wilson

Supermarketing
On tiptoe for the top shelf's
Chinese Figs in Syrup,
Miss Butterfingers

   let
       them
           slip
               and
                    they
                        hit

The Polish Bilberries,
Which hit the Californian Peaches,
Which hit the Heinz Beef Soup,
Tomato Soup, Scotch Broth,
Cream of Chicken, Baked Beans,
Baked Beans with Eight Grilled Pork Sausages,
Pepsi, Coca Cola, Lilt,
Dandelion and Burdock,
Shandy, Quosh, loose rice,
Chum, Swoop, Bounce, Trill, Smash,
Prunes, and English Plums.

'Oh!' she cried, 'My fingers are all thumbs . . .'
But, 'least said, soonest mended.'
The manager said, 'I fully intended

to take them all down in any case.'
'In any case?'
'Yes, any old case,
and stack the shelves with Christmas fare.
Will you help me?'
And then and there
Her fingers became their careful selves
In spite of her name, and they stacked the shelves

                    with
                top
            the
        to
      up
  Right

Christmas puddings, Christmas cakes,
Jars of mincemeat, stuffing-mix,
Tins of turkey, chicken, ham and mushroom,
Scampi, prawns and salmon,
Raisins, currants and sultanas,
Cherries, marzipan bananas,
Sugar mice and silver balls,
Almonds, walnuts, Brazils,
Orange slices, lemon slices,
Catherine-wheels in lacy boxes,
Cranberry sauce, brandy sauce,
Marrons glacés, petits fours,
Castor, brown and icing sugar,
Painted Eastern jars of ginger,
Cherry brandy, brandy butter,
Clove and cinnamon, vanilla,
Crisps and twiglets, chocolate coins,
Trifle sponges and meringues.

Then Miss Butterfingers crept away,
Carefully swinging the swing door,
And bolted for home without stopping.

'Mum!' she yelled as she stumbled in,
'It's time to do our Christmas shopping!'

Mincemeat

Elizabeth Gould

Sing a song of mincemeat,
Currants, raisins, spice,
Apples, sugar, nutmeg,
Everything that's nice,
Stir it with a ladle,
Wish a lovely wish,
Drop it in the middle
Of your well-filled dish,
Stir again for good luck,
Pack it all away
Tied in little jars and pots
Until
     Christmas
          Day.

The Christmas Pudding

Into the basin
put the plums,
Stir-about, stir-about,
stir-about!

Next the good
white flour comes,
Stir-about, stir-about,
stir-about!

Sugar and peel
and eggs and spice,
Stir-about, stir-about,
stir-about!

Mix them and fix them
and cook them twice,
Stir-about, stir-about,
stir-about!

Anon

A Week to Christmas

John Cotton

Sunday with six whole days to go,
How we'll endure it I don't know!

Monday the goodies are in the making,
Spice smells of pudding and mince pies a-baking.

Tuesday, dad's home late and quiet as a mouse
He smuggles packages into the house.

Wednesday's the day for decorating the tree.
Will the lights work again? We'll have to see!

Thursday's for last minute shopping and hurry,
We've never seen mum in quite such a flurry!

Friday is Christmas Eve when we'll lie awake
Trying to sleep before the day break

And that special quiet of Christmas morn
When out there somewhere Christ was born.

In the Week when Christmas Comes

Eleanor Farjeon

This is the week when Christmas comes,
   Let every pudding burst with plums,
And every tree bear dolls and drums,
   In the week when Christmas comes.

Let every hall have boughs of green,
With berries glowing in between,
   In the week when Christmas comes.

Let every doorstep have a song
Sounding the dark street along,
   In the week when Christmas comes.

Let every steeple ring a bell
With a joyful tale to tell,
   In the week when Christmas comes.

Let every night put forth a star
To show us where the heavens are,
   In the week when Christmas comes.

Let every pen enfold a lamb
Sleeping warm beside its dam,
   In the week when Christmas comes.

This is the week when Christmas comes.

Feed the Birds

The North Wind

Anon

The North Wind does blow
And we shall have snow,
And what will the robin do then,
       Poor thing?
He'll sit in a barn
And keep himself warm,
And hide his head under his wing.
       Poor thing.

Robin's Song

Rodney Bennett

Robins sang in England,
   Frost or rain or snow,
All the long December days
   Endless years ago.

Robins sang in England
   Before the Legions came,
Before our English fields were tilled
   Or England was a name.

Robins sang in England
   When forests dark and wild
Stretched across from sea to sea
   And Jesus was a child.

Listen! In the frosty dawn
   From his leafless bough
The same brave song he ever sang
   A robin's singing now.

After breakfast

Roy Fuller

I stop myself sliding a morsel
Of bacon fat into the bin.
It will do as a meal for the robin,
His legs are so terribly thin.

The Holly Tree

The leaves of the holly tree
Reach right down,
Prickly and shiny green,
To the frosty ground,

Making a spiky wall
No one can get inside
And a tower too tall
For anyone to climb.

This is a tree that keeps
Its scarlet berries out of reach
So hungry birds may eat
However hard it freezes.

Stanley Cook

Winter Birds

Leslie Norris

Most mornings now they're there,
Humped on the chestnut fence
Awaiting the regular hour
That brings me out of the shower,
Warm, pulling on my pants,
Enjoying a last yawn.
They might have been there since dawn.

And have been for all I know.
So I crumble up their bread
As a famished one or two
Hop down on to the snow —
Thrushes, all bold eye
And cream and coffee feather.
How they confront the weather!

It is habit, I suppose,
That brings these birds to wait,
And the natures that they all
So variously inherit
Show up as they strut and eat —
These starlings now, they call
Their friends to share their meal.

And when all seems to have gone
An elegant wagtail comes,
Turning his slender neck
And precise, selective beak
To feed on specks so small
They seem not there at all.
He eats the crumbs of crumbs.

But the harsh, predatory,
Scavenging, black-headed gulls
Uncertainly wheel and call,
Or balefully sit in the field.
Though fiercely hunger pulls
They will not come for the bread
And fly at the lift of my head.

But it is the gulls I hear
As I take the car down the road,
Their voices cold as winter,
Their wings grey as a cloud.
They've had nothing from my hands,
And I wish before dark fall
Some comfort for us all.

Castle Gardens, Swansea: Christmas Eve

Peter Thabit Jones

In the park, Christmas Eve,
A lady shares her lunch
With a throbbing puddle
Of pigeons at her feet.

A Change in the Weather

Anne English

Stately swans in the water
Swim and glide.
Funny ducks on the ice
Can only slip and slide.

Spill

Judith Thurman

the wind scatters
a flock of sparrows —
a handful of small change
spilled suddenly
from the cloud's pocket.

Sports . . .
and
Entertainments

Calling, calling

Wes Magee

The sky is grey
And flakes are falling.
I hear the snowmen
        Calling, calling.

Outside, it's wild.
Dad's car is stalling.
Next door my friends are
        Calling, calling.

Sliding, sledging,
And, oh, snowballing!
The winter winds are
        Calling, calling.

Freddy

Colin West

Freddy down the
Mountain skiing
Hit and killed a
Human being;
And to top this
Sad disaster,
Had to have his
Toe in plaster.

Toboggan

Colin West

To begin to toboggan, first buy a toboggan,
But don't buy too big a toboggan.
(A too big a toboggan is not a toboggan
To buy to begin to toboggan.)

The Snowman

Mother, while you were at the shops
and I was snoozing in my chair
I heard a tap at the window
saw a snowman standing there

He looked so cold and miserable
I almost could have cried
so I put the kettle on
and invited him inside

I made him a cup of cocoa
to warm the cockles of his nose
then he snuggled in front of the fire
for a cosy little doze

He lay there warm and smiling
softly counting sheep
I eavesdropped for a little while
then I too fell asleep

Seems he awoke and tiptoed out
exactly when I'm not too sure
it's a wonder you didn't see him
as you came in through the door

(oh, and by the way,
the kitten's made a puddle on the floor)

Roger McGough

Skating

from 'The Prelude'

William Wordsworth

And in the frosty season, when the sun
Was set, and visible for many a mile
The cottage windows through the twilight blazed,
I heeded not the summons: clear and loud
The village clock tolled six; I wheeled about,
Proud and exulting, like an untired horse,
That cares not for its home. — All shod with steel,
We hissed along the polished ice, in games
Confederate, imitative of the chase
And woodland pleasures, the resounding horn,
The Pack loud bellowing, and the hunted hare.

So through the darkness and the cold we flew,
And not a voice was idle; with the din,
Meanwhile, the precipices rang aloud,
The leafless trees, and every icy crag
Tinkled like iron, while the distant hills
Into the tumult sent an alien sound
Of melancholy, not unnoticed, while the stars,
Eastward, were sparkling clear, and in the West
The orange sky of evening died away.

Any Colour, as long as it's White

Moira Andrew

I left the garden winter-grey
when I went to bed last night.
While I slept a painter came and
emulsioned the whole place white.

The fence, the swing, my father's
car, everything whitewashed clean;
not a stain, not a mark, no dirty
footsteps anywhere to be seen.

I hurried into my wellies,
my woolly hat and my coat.
I stepped into the pure white garden
and with a stick I wrote

a poem on blank white paper
where the lawn was supposed to be.
Then I painted a picture all in white
— I had no choice, you see.

I sculpted a giant snowman,
white body, white head, white feet.
Then it started snowing again
and I had to beat a retreat.

All *my* artistic efforts were lost
under a brush that was full of snow
as the demon artist covered them up
in the one colour he seems to know!

Jingle Bells

James Pierpont

Dashing through the snow,
In a one-horse open sleigh;
O'er the fields we go,
Laughing all the way;
Bells on bob-tail ring,
Making spirits bright;
Oh what fun to ride and sing
A sleighing song tonight.

Jingle bells, jingle bells,
Jingle all the way;
Oh! What joy it is to ride
In a one-horse open sleigh.
Jingle bells, jingle bells,
Jingle all the way.
Oh! What joy it is to ride
In a one-horse open sleigh.

The Circus

C J Dennis

Hey, there! Hoop-la! The circus is in town!
Have you seen the elephant? Have you seen the clown?
Have you seen the dappled horse gallop round the ring?
Have you seen the acrobats on the dizzy swing?
Have you seen the tumbling men tumble up and down?
Hoop-la! Hoop-la! The circus is in town!

Hey, there! Hoop-la! Here's the circus troupe!
Here's the educated dog jumping through the hoop.
See the lady Blondin with the parasol and fan,
The lad upon the ladder and the india-rubber man.
See the joyful juggler and the boy who loops the loop.
Hey! Hey! Hey! Hey! Here's the circus troupe!

Bring on the Clowns

Bring on the clowns!
Bring on the clowns!
Clowns wearing knickers
and clowns
wearing gowns.

Tall clowns and short clowns and skinny and fat,
a flat-footed clown with a jumping-jack hat.
A clown walking under a portable shower,
getting all wet just to water a flower.
A barefoot buffoon with balloons on his toes,
a clown with a polka-dot musical nose.
Clowns wearing teapots and clowns wearing plumes,
a clown with a tail made of brushes and brooms.

A balancing clown on a wobbly wheel,
seventeen clowns in an automobile.
Two jesters on pogo sticks dressed up in kilts,
pursuing a prankster escaping on stilts.
A sad-looking clown with a face like a tramp,
a clown with his stomach lit up like a lamp.
How quickly a clown can coax smiles out of frowns!
Make way for the merriment . . . bring on the clowns!

Jack Prelutsky

Our Nativity Play

Eric Finney

It went pretty well, our Nativity play,
In front of our mums in the hall.
Though it wasn't quite perfect, our teacher Miss May
Said the slip-ups weren't noticed at all.

It's a pity the innkeeper's wife was away
With pains in her head and her tum;
Sally Ann took her part and forgot what to say —
She stood there just sucking her thumb.

Still, it wasn't too bad our Nativity show:
Our mums seemed to like it a lot
When a King dropped his casket on Joseph's big toe,
And he called him a clumsy great clot!

All the angels were great; in the whitest attire
They came on in a great ghostly group,
But Sandra's right wing fluttered clean off its wire
And her other wing started to droop.

The boss of the shepherds was Christopher Powell:
His costume was tight 'cos he's fat,
So he cut a great slit in his mum's stripy towel —
I bet he'll get walloped for that.

All the audience clapped our Nativity play;
I don't know what that kid in the choir meant
When he said that he thought that our teacher Miss May
Ought to think about early retirement.

Well, there were a few slip-ups perhaps on the day,
But they just didn't matter at all
When Mary sang Jesus to sleep in the hay
And we all gathered round in the stall.

Oh no you don't! Oh yes we do!

Peter Little

For our Christmas treat
dad took me and four friends
to see 'Cinderella' in town.
There was loud music, excitement,
and sweets wrapped in crackly paper
when the theatre lights went down.

During the interval
we tucked into ice-creams
and swigged bottles of fizzy drink.
On stage, mice and a pumpkin
turned into a coach and horses
quicker than you could blink.

Then, wearing wigs of shocking pink,
the Ugly Sisters waddled on.
Their noses were fluorescent blue.
'Oh no you don't!' they shouted.
'Oh yes we do!' we replied. 'OH NO YOU DON'T!'
'OH YES WE DO! *OH YES WE DO!!*'

When it was over we filed out
and squashed into the back seat
of dad's big old car.
Jolting, we headed home.
Overhead the sky was jet black.
Look, the Plough . . . and the North Star.

Suddenly my friend said,
'Jane's feeling ill.
I think she's going to be sick!'
'Oh no she isn't!' dad muttered grimly.
'Oh yes she is!' we chorused.
'Stop the car, QUICK! *QUICK!!*'

Uuggghh!

Winter
Weather

White December

What colour is December?
White do you say?
Looking from your window
On a frosty day.

What colour is December?
White do you say?
Jumping into snowdrifts
Wind has piled your way.

What colour is December?
Think before you say;
It's sparkling as the tinsel,
Red as berries bright,
Glossy green as Christmas trees
And starry as the night.

Anne English

Riddle

John Cotton

I work while you sleep,
Needing no light to etch windows
Or elaborate leaf or branch.
Without colour my wonder is
My patterns within patterns
Growing like crisp stars.
Look, but do not touch,
Your warmth is my end.

(Answer: *Frost*)

Winter Days

Gareth Owen

Biting air
Winds blow
City streets
Under snow

Noses red
Lips sore
Runny eyes
Hands raw

Chimneys smoke
Cars crawl
Piled snow
On garden wall

Slush in gutters
Ice in lanes
Frosty patterns
On window panes

Morning call
Lift up head
Nipped by winter
Stay in bed.

In the Wood

Cold winter's in the wood,
 I saw him pass
Crinkling up fallen leaves
 Along the grass.

Bleak winter's in the wood,
 The birds have flown
Leaving the naked trees
 Shivering alone.

King Winter's in the wood
 I saw him go
Crowned with a coronet
 Of crystal snow.

Eileen Mathias

Windy Nights

Rodney Bennett

Rumbling in the chimneys,
   Rattling at the doors,
Round the roofs and round the roads
   The rude wind roars;
Raging through the darkness,
   Raving through the trees,
Racing off again across
   The great grey seas.

Stopping by Woods on a Snowy Evening

Robert Frost

Whose woods these are I think I know.
His house is in the village though;
He will not see me stopping here
To watch his woods fill up with snow.

My little horse must think it queer
To stop without a farmhouse near
Between the woods and frozen lake
The darkest evening of the year.

He gives his harness bells a shake
To ask if there is some mistake.
The only other sound's the sweep
Of easy wind and downy flake.

The woods are lovely, dark and deep,
But I have promises to keep,
And miles to go before I sleep,
And miles to go before I sleep.

A Week of Winter Weather

Wes Magee

On Monday icy rains poured down
And flooded drains all over town.

Tuesday's gales rent elm and ash:
Dead branches came down with a crash.

On Wednesday bursts of hail and sleet.
No one walked along our street.

Thursday stood out clear and calm
But the sun was paler than my arm.

Friday's frost that bit your ears
Was cold enough to freeze your tears.

Saturday's sky was ghostly grey.
We smashed ice on the lake today.

Christmas Eve was Sunday and
Snow fell like foam across the land.

The Night before Christmas

from **The Christmas Tree**

Put out the lights now!
Look at the Tree, the rough tree dazzled
In oriole plumes of flame,
Tinselled with twinkling frost fire, tasselled
With stars and moons — the same
That yesterday hid in the spinney and had no fame
Till we put out the lights now!

C Day Lewis

Christmas Stocking

Eleanor Farjeon

What will go into the Christmas Stocking
While the clock on the mantelpiece goes tick-tocking?
    An orange, a penny,
    Some sweets, not too many,
    A trumpet, a dolly,
    A sprig of green holly,
    A book and a top,
    And a grocery shop,
    Some beads in a box,
    An ass and an ox,
    And a lamb, plain and good,
    All whittled in wood,
    A white sugar dove,
    A handful of love,
    Another of fun,
    And it's very near done –
    A big silver star
    On top – there you are!
Come morning you'll wake to the clock's tick-tocking,
And that's what you'll find in the Christmas Stocking.

At Nine of the Night I opened my Door

Charles Causley

At nine of the night I opened my door
That stands midway between moor and moor,
And all around me, silver-bright,
I saw that the world had turned to white.

Thick was the snow on field and hedge
And vanished was the river-sedge,
Where winter skilfully had wound
A shining scarf without a sound.

And as I stood and gazed my fill
A stable-boy came down the hill.
With every step I saw him take
Flew at his heel a puff of flake.

His brow was whiter than the hoar,
A beard of freshest snow he wore,
And round about him, snowflake starred,
A red horse-blanket from the yard.

In a red cloak I saw him go,
His back was bent, his step was slow,
And as he laboured through the cold
He seemed a hundred winters old.

I stood and watched the snowy head,
The whiskers white, the cloak of red.
'A Merry Christmas!' I heard him cry.
'The same to you, old friend,' said I.

The Twenty-Fourth of December

Anon

The clock ticks slowly, slowly in the hall,
And slower and more slow the long hours crawl;
It seems as though today
Would never pass away;
The clock ticks slowly, s-l-o-w-l-y in the hall.

Unable to Sleep

Peter Thabit Jones

Unable to sleep,
I creep downstairs;
Nothing stirs
In this room-arrested darkness.

I pull the curtain
And peep through the window;
Frost, like a memory of snow,
Whitens my garden,
The roof of my neighbour's car,
The park beyond.

The coldness of winter covers my thoughts.

Behind me, the clock
Ticks into the ghost of time,
Ticks into my head,
Ticks into silence.

Questions on Christmas Eve

Wes Magee

But *how* can his reindeer fly without wings?
Jets on their hooves? That's plain cheating!
And *how* can he climb down the chimney pot
  When we've got central heating?

You say it's all magic and I shouldn't ask
About Santa on Christmas Eve.
But I'm confused by the stories I've heard;
  I don't know what to believe.

I said that I'd sit up in bed all night long
To see if he really would call.
But I fell fast asleep, woke up after dawn
  As something banged in the hall.

I saw my sock crammed with apples and sweets;
There were parcels piled high near the door.
Jingle bells tinkled far off in the dark:
  One snowflake shone on the floor.

A Gift from the Stars

John Rice

On Christmas Eve, on the first chime of midnight,
the Christmas King and the Queen of Christmas
take the new moon, sharp as a blade,
and slit the thin paper sky.

They help each other wrap up the frosty stars
in the night's dark blue wrapping paper;
the Queen stretches out her sparkling hand
and grasps a passing comet to use as a gift tag.

The Queen of Christmas and the Christmas King
then take their present on a long journey:
    they slide past the icy meteorites,
    they glide between the glassy suns,
    they slink in and out of cosmic clouds,
    they skim the outer edges of planets' rings
making their way through the caves and caverns of
        space
to this shining Earth
to this cold country
to this snowy town
to this still street
to this sleeping house
to this quiet bedroom
to this soft bed
and place their sky gift on your pillow.

And ping!
the second you open your eyes on Christmas morn
the parcel bursts open without a sound
and showers you with frosty stars
that zing and spin and melt and split and vanish
to become minuscule molecules of happiness.

And because children wake up so early
on Christmas Day (usually while it's still dark)
they never see this remarkable scientific phenomenon.

A Visit from St Nicholas

Clement Moore

'Twas the night before Christmas, when all through the
          house
Not a creature was stirring, not even a mouse:
The stockings were hung by the chimney with care,
In hopes that St Nicholas soon would be there;
The children were nestled all snug in their beds
While visions of sugar-plums danced in their heads;
And Mamma in her 'kerchief, and I in my cap,
Had just settled down for a long winter's nap,
When out on the lawn there arose such a clatter,
I sprang from my bed to see what was the matter.
Away to the window I flew like a flash,
Tore open the shutters and threw up the sash.
The moon on the breast of the new-fallen snow

Gave a lustre of midday to objects below,
When, what to my wondering eyes did appear,
But a miniature sleigh and eight tiny reindeer,
With a little old driver, so lively and quick,
I knew in a moment it must be St Nick.
More rapid than eagles his coursers they came,
And he whistled, and shouted, and called them by
                name:
'Now, Dasher! now, Dancer! now, Prancer and Vixen!
On, Comet! on, Cupid! on, Donder and Blitzen!
To the top of the porch! to the top of the wall!
Now dash away! dash away! dash away all!'
As dry leaves that before the wild hurricane fly,
When they meet with an obstacle, mount to the sky,
So up to the housetop the coursers they flew,
With a sleigh full of toys, and St Nicholas too.
And then, in a twinkling, I heard on the roof
The prancing and pawing of each little hoof.
As I drew in my head, and was turning around,
Down the chimney St Nicholas came with a bound.
He was dressed all in fur, from his head to his foot,
And his clothes were all tarnished with ashes and soot;
A bundle of toys he had flung on his back,
And he looked like a pedlar just opening his pack.
His eyes — how they twinkled! his dimples, how merry!
His cheeks were like roses, his nose like a cherry!
His droll little mouth was drawn up like a bow,
And the beard on his chin was as white as the snow;
The stump of a pipe he held tight in his teeth,
And the smoke, it encircled his head like a wreath;
He had a broad face and a round little belly
That shook, when he laughed, like a bowl full of jelly.
He was chubby and plump, a right jolly old elf,

And I laughed when I saw him, in spite of myself;
A wink of his eye and a twist of his head,
Soon gave me to know I had nothing to dread;
He spoke not a word, but went straight to his work,
And filled all the stockings; then turned with a jerk,
And laying his finger aside of his nose,
And giving a nod, up the chimney he rose.
He sprang to his sleigh, to his team gave a whistle,
And away they all flew like the down of a thistle.

But I heard him exclaim, ere he drove out of sight,
    'Happy Christmas to all,
    And to all a good-night!'

Merry Christmas!

Christmas Morning

Peter Thabit Jones

I wake on Christmas morning,
My stocking on my bed;
Christmas Eve has come and gone:
And Santa Claus has fled!

My presents all around me:
A bike! A ball to throw!
I look through the window pane,
At footsteps in the snow.

An old Christmas Greeting

Anon

Sing hey!
Sing hey!
For Christmas Day;
Twine mistletoe and holly.
For friendship glows
In winter snows,
And so let's all be jolly!

A Bunch of Holly

Christina Rossetti

But give me holly, bold and jolly,
Honest, prickly, shining holly;
Pluck me holly leaf and berry
For the day when I make merry.

The Computer's first Christmas Card

Edwin Morgan

```
jollymerry
hollyberry
jollyberry
merryholly
happyjolly
jollyjelly
jellybelly
bellymerry
hollyheppy
jollyMolly
merryJerry
```

merryHarry
hoppyBarry
heppyJarry
boppyheppy
berryjorry
jorryjolly
moppyjelly
Mollymerry
Jerryjolly
bellyboppy
jorryhoppy
hollymoppy
Barrymerry
Jarryheppy
happyboppy
boppyjolly
jollymerry
merrymerry
merrymerry
merryChris
ammerryasa
Chrismerry
asMERRYCHR
YSANTHEMUM

Christmas Morning

Open the stocking,
what's in there?
Five hazelnuts, an apple,
a tangerine, a pear.

Untie the ribbons,
what do you spy?
A pencil and a hanky,
a freshly-baked mince pie.

Take off the wrappings,
what can it be?
A clockwork car, a storybook,
a game of chess for me.

Look by the fireside,
what is that?
A box of paints, a jigsaw,
a red wool stripy hat.

Peep through the curtains,
who goes there?
Mary and her Baby,
and the Christmas star.

Judith Nicholls

Christmas Presents

Eric James

Have you ever noticed how grown-ups give each other
            presents?
There's no mystery in it, and not a lot of fun.

Every year Grandma gets a tin of talcum powder.
She always says, 'Ah my favourite!'
Even before she opens the wrapping.
Grandpa always says, 'Well, I know what's in here.
   It's two pairs of socks. Just what I wanted!'

This year, Auntie Vi had an umbrella
   in an umbrella-shaped parcel.
I mean, it *looked* just like an umbrella.
And, before Auntie Vi pulled the paper off,
   she said to Mum, 'It will match that new coat of mine.'

As for Mum and Dad, they just sat there and said,
'We've given each other a joint present this year.
   It's a digital clock-radio for our bedroom.'
Do you know, they didn't even bother to wrap it
   up and put it under the tree!

At the end, when everything had been given out,
Mum said, 'We mustn't forget the gift vouchers
   from Debbie and Jim. We sent them a cheque
   for the same amount. We always do.'
I call that a bit unimaginative, don't you?

Maybe, when you come to think about it,
Grown-ups need Father Christmas far more
    than children do.

Cousin Bert

Shelagh McGee

Cousin Bert
Has a very nice shirt
With Christmas trees
And mountains.

It's striped and checked
And all bedecked
With polka dots
And fountains.

The Turkey

Richard Digance

Turkeys don't like Christmas
which may come as no surprise.
They say why don't human beings
pick on people their own size.
To sit beside potatoes
in an oven can't be fun,
so a turkey is quite justified
to feel he's being done.

Christmas Alphabet

John Fairfax

Apple crumble
Banana flan
Cut-and-come-again cake
Dumplings
Eclairs
Fudge
Gooseberries
Ham
Ice-cream
Jam
Kippers
Lemon curd
Mince pies
Nuts
Oranges
Pickles
Quince
Rice
Sausages
Trifle and turkey
Uglifruit
Veal
Welsh rarebit
Xmas pudding
Yorkie bars
    Eat all these at Christmas
    and you'll be
Zick!

Snapdragon

Anon

Here he comes with flaming bowl,
Don't he mean to take his toll,
   Snip! Snap! Dragon.
Take care you don't take too much,
Be not greedy in your clutch,
   Snip! Snap! Dragon.

With his blue and lapping tongue
Many of you will be stung,
   Snip! Snap! Dragon.
For he snaps at all that comes
Snatching at his feast of plums,
   Snip! Snap! Dragon.

But old Christmas makes him come,
Though he looks so fee! fo! fum!
   Snip! Snap! Dragon.
Don't ever fear him, but be bold,
Out he goes, his flames are cold,
   Snip! Snap! Dragon.

Christmas Day

Brian Moses

It was waking early & making a din.
It was knowing that for the next twenty minutes
    I'd never be quite so excited again.
It was singing the last verse of
    'O Come all Ye Faithful', the one that's
    only meant to be sung on Christmas Day.
It was lighting a fire in the unused room
    & a draught that blew back woodsmoke
    into our faces.
It was lunch & a full table,
    & dad repeating how he'd once eaten his
    off the bonnet of a lorry in Austria.
It was keeping quiet for the Queen
    & Gran telling that one about children
    being seen but not heard.
    (As if we could get a word in edgeways
    once she started!)
It was 'Monopoly' & me out to cheat the Devil
    to be first to reach Mayfair.
It was, 'Just a small one for the lad,'
    & dad saying, 'We don't want him getting tiddly.'
It was aunts assaulting the black piano,
    & me keeping clear of mistletoe
    in case they trapped me.
It was pinning a tail on the donkey,
    & nuts that wouldn't crack
    & crackers that pulled apart but didn't bang.

And then when the day was almost gone,
   it was dad on the stairs,
   on his way to bed,
   & one of us saying:
            'You've forgotten to take your hat off . . .'
   & the purple or pink or orange paper
   still crowning his head.

Christmas Day Walk

Wes Magee

Down to the end of our housing estate,
Across fields to Hanging Man's Wood
Where skeletal trees stand black and bare
And the chilled air freezes your blood.

In wellington boots we crunch through the snow,
Watch a magpie flutter and squawk.
A fluffed-up thrush trembles on a thin twig
And the sky is grey as wet chalk.

At the edge of the wood we stand stone-still
As moth snowflakes start to whirl down.
There are no cars on the roads, not a sound
As Christmas Day blankets the town.

The Father Christmas on the Cake

Colin West

For fifty weeks I've languished
Upon the cupboard shelf,
Forgotten and uncared for,
I've muttered to myself.
But now the year is closing,
And Christmastime is here,
They dust me down and tell me
To show a little cheer.
Between the plaster snowman
And little glassy lake
They stand me in the middle
Of some ice-covered cake,
And for a while there's laughter,
But as the week wears on,
They cut up all the landscape
Till every scrap is gone.
Then with the plaster snowman
And little lake of glass
I'm banished to the cupboard
For one more year to pass.

The Christmas Party

We're going to have a party
   And a lovely Christmas tea,
And flags and lighted candles
   Upon the Christmas tree!

And silver balls and lanterns
   Tied on with golden string,
Will hide among the branches
   By little bells that ring.

And then there will be crackers
And caps and hats and toys,
A Christmas cake and presents
For all the girls and boys.

Adeline White

The Magic Show

Vernon Scannell

After a feast of sausage-rolls,
Sandwiches of various meats,
Jewelled jellies, brimming bowls
Of chocolate ice and other treats,
We children played at Blind Man's Buff,
Hide and Seek, Pin-the-tail-on-Ned,
And then — when we'd had just enough
Of party-games — we all were led
Into another room to see
The Magic Show. The wizard held
A wand of polished ebony.
His white-gloved, flickering hands compelled
The rapt attention of us all.
He conjured from astonished air
A living pigeon and a fall
Of paper snowflakes; made us stare
Bewildered as a playing card —
Unlike a leopard — changed its spots
And disappeared. He placed some starred
And satin scarves in silver pots,
Withdrew them as plain bits of rag,
Then swallowed them before our eyes.
But soon we felt attention flag
And found delighted, first surprise
Had withered like a wintry leaf;
And, when the tricks were over, we
Applauded, yet felt some relief,
And left the party willingly.

'Goodnight,' we said, 'and thank you for
The lovely time we've had.' Outside,
The freezing night was still. We saw
Above our heads the slow clouds stride
Across the vast unswallowable skies;
White, graceful gestures of the moon,
The stars' intent and glittering eyes,
And, gleaming like a silver spoon,
The frosty path to lead us home.
Our breath hung blossoms on unseen
Boughs of air as we paused there,
And we forgot that we had been
Pleased briefly by that conjuror,
Could not recall his tricks, or face,
Bewitched and awed, as now we were,
By magic of the common place.

Christmas Thank You's

Mick Gowar

Dear Auntie
Oh, what a nice jumper
I've always adored powder blue
and fancy thinking of
orange and pink
for the stripes
how clever of you!

Dear Uncle
The soap is
terrific
So
useful
and such a kind thought and
how did you guess that
I'd just used the last of
the soap that last Christmas brought

Dear Gran
Many thanks for the hankies
Now I really can't wait for the 'flu
and the daisies embroidered
in red round the 'M'
for Michael
how
thoughtful of you!

Dear Cousin
What socks!
and the same sort you wear
so you must be
the last word in style
and I'm certain you're right that the
luminous green
will make me stand out a mile

Dear Sister
I quite understand your concern
it's a risk sending jam in the post
But I think I've pulled out
all the big bits
of glass
so it won't taste too sharp
spread on toast

Dear Grandad
Don't fret
I'm delighted
So *don't* think your gift will
offend
I'm not at all hurt
that you gave up this year
and just sent me
a fiver
to spend

Pictures on the Lawn

Eric Finney

Boxing Day at home
(where the boxing comes in
I can't guess):
Work to be done
Clearing up
The Christmas Day mess.
Mum giving orders
(dad's still asleep),
'Just pop that waste
down to the compost heap.
Do you good
To get some fresh air.'
So I grub under the sink —
It's a shambles down there:
Wine bottles, turkey bones,
Christmas wrapping paper —
Torn off quickly yesterday
In the present-opening caper.
I heave out the compost bucket —
Which smells:
Banana skins, date stones,
Peelings, nutshells,
Tangerine and satsuma skins,
Mouldy grapes,
Various stuff that's been
Scraped off plates.
Then I'm off down the garden
Bucket swinging;

Frost,
Brilliant sun,
The morning singing;
Yesterday's puddles
Turned to glass,
And me crunching prints
In the frosty grass.
Upend the bucket
On dad's neat stack —
And notice the lawn
As I set off back:
Where the sun's falling bright
Frost's gone from the grass,
It's slithery and green
As I pass;
Where the low sun casts shadows
There's still frost on the lawn,
And in grey shapes on green
I see perfectly drawn:
Our garden fence,
Real rickety,
With all its ups and downs;
A tall shrub and a baggy one —
Just like a pair of clowns;
Our shed,
Which dad won't fix,
Dilapidated, floppy,
Projected neatly on the grass —
A perfect frosty copy.
And the sight of all that
Makes me feel real good;
Rush indoors to mum,
Who's heating up

Christmas pud.
'There's pictures on the lawn, mum;
They'll soon fade though —
Come and see.'
And she smiled and took her pinny off
And came and looked with me.

A New Star

High in the Heaven

Charles Causley

High in the heaven
A gold star burns
Lighting our way
As the great world turns.

Silver the frost
It shines on the stem
As we now journey
To Bethlehem.

White is the ice
At our feet as we tread,
Pointing a path
To the manger-bed.

Long, Long Ago

Anon

Wind through the olive trees
Softly did blow,
Round little Bethlehem
Long, long ago.

Sheep on the hillside lay
Whiter than snow,
Shepherds were watching them
Long, long ago.

Then from the happy sky
Angels bent low,
Singing their songs of joy
Long, long ago.

For in a manger-bed
Cradled we know,
Christ came to Bethlehem
Long, long ago.

The Carol of the Poor Children

We are the poor children, come out to see the sights
On this day of all days, on this night of nights:
The stars in merry parties are dancing in the sky,
A fine star, a new star, is shining on high!

We are the poor children, our lips are frosty blue,
We cannot sing our carol as well as rich folk do;
Our bellies are so empty we have no singing voice,
But this night of all nights good children must rejoice.

We do rejoice, we do rejoice, as hard as we can try,
A fine star, a new star is shining in the sky!
And while we sing our carol, we think of the delight
The happy kings and shepherds make in Bethlehem
        tonight.

Are we naked, mother, and are we starving-poor —
Oh, see what gifts the kings have brought outside the
      stable door.
Are we cold, mother, the ass will give us his hay
To make the manger warm and keep the cruel winds
      away.

We are the poor children, but not so poor who sing
Our carol with our voiceless hearts to greet the new-
      born king:
On this night of all nights, when in the frosty sky
A new star, a kind star is shining on high!

Richard Middleton

The Barn

Elizabeth Coatsworth

'I am tired of this barn,' said the colt.
'And every day it snows.
Outside there's no grass any more
And icicles grow on my nose.
I am tired of hearing the cows
Breathing and talking together.
I am sick of these clucking hens.
I *hate* stables and winter weather!'

'Hush, little colt,' said the mare,
'And a story I will tell
Of a barn like this one of ours
And the wonders that there befell.
It was weather much like this,
And the beasts stood as we stand now
In the warm good dark of the barn —
A horse, and an ass, and a cow.'

'And sheep?' asked the colt. 'Yes, sheep.
And a pig, and a goat, and a hen.
All of the beasts of the barnyard,
The usual servants of men.
And into their midst came a lady
And she was cold as death,
But the animals leaned over her
And made her warm with their breath.

'There was her baby born
And laid to sleep in the hay,
While music flooded the rafters
And the barn was as light as day.
And angels and kings and shepherds
Came to worship the babe from afar,
But we looked at him first of all creatures
By the bright strange light of a star!'

The Shepherds' Song

Charles Causley

I am a shepherd,
My name is Ben,
I've shepherded
Three-score years and ten.
Spring, summer, autumn,
Winter, too!
The years and the seasons
How they flew!
Now my nose is fire
And my hair is frost,
But never a sheep or lamb
I lost.

I am a shepherd,
My name is Dan,
In seven more years
I'll be a man,
But ever since I
Could stand or run
I've shepherded sheep
In rain and sun.
I've shepherded sheep
On hill and moor
As my father did,
And his before.

I am a shepherd,
My name is John,
I work with my father
And my son.
In forty years
Of cold and heat,
I never have lost
A lamb or sheep.
In weather gold,
In weather grey,
No sheep or lamb
Was stolen away.

One Shepherd

Peter Thabit Jones

And one shepherd, full of himself,
Did not go.
He remained in the field,
Feeling the black winter
As bitter and cold as his thoughts;
While the other shepherds
Were humbled by the warmth,
Like sunlight,
Surrounding the world's child.

Kings came Riding

Kings came riding,
One, two, and three,
Over the desert
And over the sea.

One in a ship
With a silver mast;
The fishermen wondered
As he went past.

One on a horse
With a saddle of gold;
The children came running
To behold.

One came walking,
  Over the sand,
With a casket of treasure
  Held in his hand.

All the people
  Said, 'where go they?'
But the Kings went forward
  All through the day.

Night came on
  As those Kings went by;
They shone like the gleaming
  Stars in the sky.

Charles Williams

The Evening Star

Guillaume Apollinaire

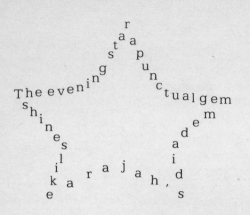

The evening star shines like a rajah, punctual gem aids a maid's

Letter from Egypt

Moira Andrew

Dear Miriam,
                Just a line
to let you know how things
are with us & of course to
thank you (& your good man)
for all you did for us — &
at your busiest time too
what with the census &
everything. I was quite
exhausted & the baby was
beginning to make himself
felt. If it hadn't been
for your help that night
my baby might have died.

        Good of you
to put up with all our
visitors — who'd have
thought, six scruffy
shepherds up & leaving
their sheep like that?
& didn't they ever smell?
Still they were good-
hearted & they meant well.
I hope they brought some
extra trade to the inn.
They looked in need of
a hot drink & a meal.

          & what about
those Kings, Miriam? Kneeling
there in their rich robes
& all? & me in nothing but
my old blue dress! Joseph
said not to worry, it was
Jesus they'd come to see.
Real gentlemen *they* were.
But what funny things to
give a baby — gold & myrrh
& frankincense. That's men
all over! It wouldn't cross
their minds to bring a shawl!

          Sorry we left
so suddenly. No time for
good-byes with King Herod on
the warpath! We had to take
the long way home & I'm so
tired of looking at sand!
Joseph has picked up a few
jobs mending this & that so
we're managing quite well.
Jesus grows bonnier every
day & thrives on this way
of life, but I can't wait
to see Nazareth again.

                 Love to all
                 at the inn,

                 Mary

Winter Tales

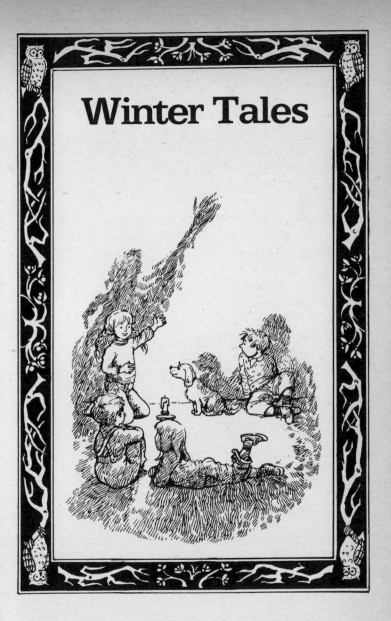

The Boy who Laughed at Santa Claus

Ogden Nash

In Baltimore there lived a boy.
He wasn't anybody's joy.
Although his name was Jabez Dawes,
His character was full of flaws.
In school he never led his classes,
He hid old ladies' reading glasses,
His mouth was open when he chewed,
And elbows to the table glued.
He stole the milk of hungry kittens,
And walked through doors marked NO ADMITTANCE.
He said he acted thus because
There wasn't any Santa Claus.
Another trick that tickled Jabez
Was crying 'Boo!' at little babies.
He brushed his teeth, they said in town,
Sideways instead of up and down.

Yet people pardoned every sin,
And viewed his antics with a grin,
Till they were told by Jabez Dawes,
'There isn't any Santa Claus!'
Deploring how he did behave,
His parents swiftly sought their grave.
They hurried through the portals pearly,
And Jabez left the funeral early.

Like whooping cough, from child to child,
He sped to spread the rumour wild:
'Sure as my name is Jabez Dawes
There isn't any Santa Claus!'
Slunk like a weasel or a marten
Through nursery and kindergarten
Whispering low to every tot
'There isn't any, no there's not!'

The children wept all Christmas Eve
And Jabez chortled up his sleeve.
No infant dared hang up his stocking
For fear of Jabez' ribald mocking.
He sprawled on his untidy bed,
Fresh malice dancing in his head,
When presently with scalp a-tingling,
Jabez heard a distant jingling;
He heard the crunch of sleigh and hoof
Crisply alighting on the roof.

What good to rise and bar the door?
A shower of soot was on the floor.
What was beheld by Jabez Dawes?
The fireplace full of Santa Claus!
Then Jabez fell upon his knees
With cries of 'Don't', and 'Pretty please'.
He howled, 'I don't know where you read it,
But anyhow, I never said it!'
'Jabez,' replied the angry saint,
'It isn't I, it's you who ain't.
Although there is a Santa Claus,
There isn't any Jabez Dawes!'
Said Jabez then with impudent vim,

'Oh yes there is; and I am him!
Your magic don't scare me, it doesn't' —
And suddenly he found he wasn't!

From grimy feet to grimy locks,
Jabez became a Jack-in-the-Box,
An ugly toy with springs unsprung,
For ever sticking out his tongue.
The neighbours heard his mournful squeal;
They searched for him, but not with zeal.
No trace was found of Jabez Dawes,
Which led to thunderous applause,
And people drank a loving cup
And went and hung their stockings up.

All you who sneer at Santa Claus,
Beware the fate of Jabez Dawes,
The saucy boy who mocked the saint.
Donder and Blitzen licked off his paint.

The Frozen Man

Kit Wright

Out at the edge of town
where black trees

crack their fingers
in the icy wind

and hedges freeze
on their shadows

and the breath of cattle,
still as boulders,

hangs in rags
under the rolling moon,

a man is walking
alone:

on the coal-black road
his cold

feet
ring

and
ring.

Here in a snug house
at the heart of town

the fire is burning
red and yellow and gold:

you can hear the warmth
like a sleeping cat

breathe softly
in every room.

When the frozen man
comes to your door,

let him in,
let him in,
let him in.

Innocent's Song

Charles Causley

Who's that knocking on the window,
Who's that standing at the door,
What are all those presents
Lying on the kitchen floor?

Who is the smiling stranger
With hair as white as gin,
What is he doing with the children
And who could have let him in?

Why has he rubies on his fingers,
A cold, cold crown on his head,
Why, when he caws his carol,
Does the salty snow run red?

Why does he ferry my fireside
As a spider on a thread,
His fingers made of fuses
And his tongue of gingerbread?

Why does the world before him
Melt in a million suns,
Why do his yellow, yearning eyes
Burn like saffron buns?

Watch where he comes walking
Out of the Christmas flame,
Dancing, double-talking;

Herod is his name.

Ghosts

Kit Wright

That's right. Sit down and talk to me.
What do you want to talk about?

Ghosts. You were saying that you believe in them.
Yes, they exist, without a doubt.

What, bony white nightmares that rattle and glow?
No, just spirits that come and go.

I've never heard such a load of rubbish.
Never mind, one day you'll know.

What makes you so sure?

I said:
What makes you so sure?

Hey,
Where did you go?

Last of the Family

Leonard Clark

On cold December nights
I remember long ago,
the sky, a maze of lights,
bright stars and moonlit snow.

And shivering birds in trees
piping a few soft notes,
the winds enough to freeze
the songs within their throats.

And in the old farmhouse,
only the tomcat's purr,
a hidden, scratching mouse,
a fire of crackling fir.

My gathered family there,
happy with time and place,
of winter unaware,
contentment on each face.

But now I sit alone,
keep company with the dead,
the future not yet known,
and all but memory fled.

They do not feel the chill,
nor care the weather bites,
but whisper to me still
on cold December nights.

The Mistletoe Bough

Thomas Haynes Bayly

The mistletoe hung in the castle hall,
The holly branch shone on the old oak wall:
And the baron's relations were blithe and gay,
And keeping their Christmas holiday.
The baron beheld with a father's pride
His beautiful child, young Lovell's bride;
While she with her bright eyes seemed to be
The star of the goodly company.

'I'm weary of dancing now,' she cried;
'Here tarry a moment — I'll hide — I'll hide!
And Lovell be sure you are first to trace
The clue to my secret lurking place.'
Away she ran — and her friends began
Each tower to search, and each nook to scan;
And young Lovell cried, 'Oh where do you hide?
I'm lonesome without you, my own dear bride.'

They sought her that night! and they sought her next
          day!
And they sought her in vain when a week passed away!
In the highest — the lowest — the loneliest spot,
Young Lovell sought wildly — but found her not.
And years flew by, and their grief at last
Was told as a sorrowful tale long past;
And when Lovell appeared, the children cried,
'See! the old man weeps for his beautiful bride.'

At length an oak chest, that had long lain hid,
Was found in the castle — they raised the lid —
And a skeleton form lay mouldering there,
In the bridal wreath of that lady fair!
Oh! sad was her fate! — in sportive jest
She hid from her lord in the old oak chest.
It closed with a spring! — and dreadful doom,
The bride lay clasped in her living tomb!

The Dance of the Thirteen Skeletons

Jack Prelutsky

In a snow-enshrouded graveyard
gripped by winter's bitter chill,
not a single soul is stirring,
all is silent, all is still
till a distant bell tolls midnight
and the spirits work their will.

For emerging from their coffins
buried deep beneath the snow,
thirteen bony apparitions
now commence their spectral show,
and they gather in the moonlight
undulating as they go.

And they'll dance in their bones,
in their bare bare bones,
with the click and the clack
and the chitter and the chack
and the clatter and the chatter
of their bare bare bones.

They shake their flimsy shoulders
and they flex their fleshless knees
and they nod their skulls in greeting
in the penetrating breeze
as they form an eerie circle
near the gnarled and twisted trees.

They link their spindly fingers
as they promenade around
casting otherworldly shadows
on the silver-mantled ground
and their footfalls in the snowdrift
make a soft, susurrous sound.

And they dance in their bones,
in their bare bare bones,
with the click and the clack
and the chitter and the chack
and the clatter and the chatter
of their bare bare bones.

The thirteen grinning skeletons
continue on their way
as to strains of soundless music
they begin to swing and sway
and they circle ever faster
in their ghastly roundelay.

Faster, faster ever faster
and yet faster now they race,
winding, whirling, ever swirling
in the frenzy of their pace
and they shimmer in the moonlight
as they spin themselves through space.

And they dance in their bones,
in their bare bare bones,
with the click and the clack
and the chitter and the chack
and the clatter and the chatter
of their bare bare bones.

Then as quickly as it started
their nocturnal dance is done
for the bell that is their signal
loudly tolls the hour of one
and they bow to one another
in their bony unison.

Then they vanish to their coffins
by their ghostly thoroughfare
and the emptiness of silence
once more fills the frosted air
and the snows that mask their footprints
show no sign that they were there.

But they danced in their bones,
in their bare bare bones,
with the click and the clack
and the chitter and the chack
and the clatter and the chatter
of their bare bare bones.

How many Miles to Mylor?

A L Rowse

How many miles to Mylor
   By frost and candle-light:
How long before I arrive there,
   This mild December night?

I mounted the hill to Mylor
   Through the thick woods of Carclew,
A clock struck the three-quarters,
   And suddenly a cock crew.

At the cross-roads on the hill-top
   The snow lay on the ground,
In the quick air and the stillness,
   No movement and no sound.

'Who is it?' said a voice from the bushes
   Beneath the rowan tree;
'Who is it?' my mouth re-echoed,
   My heart went out of me.

I cannot tell what queerness
   There lay around Carclew;
Nor whatever stirred in the hedges
   When an owl replied 'Who-whoo'.

A lamp in a lone cottage,
   A face in a window-frame,
Above the snow a wicket:
   A house without a name.

How many miles to Mylor
   This dark December night:
And shall I ever arrive there
   By frost or candle-light?

The Winter Dragon

The wind was scattering flakes of snow
As if it were tearing up the sky
When the hero fastened on his sword
Engraved with spells along both sides.

The snowflakes tumbled over each other
As if they were fleeing in fear
When the hero put his helmet on
And shouldered his long, broad-bladed spear.

Men were bringing the sheep and cattle in
That were freezing to death in the fields
When the hero hung his horn from his neck
And took up his seven-layered shield.

He made his way up the mountain
Through hollows where snowdrifts lay
And over the bare black knuckles of rock
Where the wind had blown the snow away.

And there in a cave on the mountain top
Was the snow-white dragon in its icy hole,
Scaled with ice, bearded with icicles
And breathing out, not flames, but cold.

The hero's shield grew heavy with ice.
He hid from its breath and sounded his horn;
Like shooting flames the blade of his spear
And the blade of his sword began to burn.

The freezing dragon caught fire
And burnt among melting snow;
From the ground that was warmed by its cinders
The Spring flowers began to grow.

Stanley Cook

Index of poets

Index of first lines

135

Acknowledgements

For permission to reprint copyright material the Editor is
indebted to:

Moira Andrew for 'Any colour, as long as it's White' and 'Letter
from Egypt'.
Angus and Robertson (UK) Ltd. for 'The circus' from *C.J. Dennis'
Book for Kids* by C.J. Dennis.
Associated Book Publishers (UK) Ltd. and Methuen Children's
Books for 'Furry bear' from *Now we are six* by A.A. Milne.
Mrs Catherine Barnes and Mrs Margaret Mechau for 'On a night of
snow' from *Night and the cat* by Elizabeth Coatsworth.
A. & C. Black (Publishers) Ltd. for 'Dance of the thirteen skeletons'
from *Nightmares: Poems to trouble your sleep* by Jack
Prelutsky.
Curtis Brown Ltd. for 'The boy who laughed at Santa Claus' from
Parents keep out by Ogden Nash.
Jonathan Cape Ltd. and the Executors of the Estate of C. Day Lewis
for the extract from 'The Christmas Tree' from *Collected Poems,
1954* by C. Day Lewis. Jonathan Cape Ltd. and the Estate of
Robert Frost for 'Stopping by woods on a snowy evening' from
The poetry of Robert Frost edited by Edward Latham.
Carcanet Press Ltd. for 'The computer's first Christmas card' from
Poems of thirty years by Edwin Morgan.
Century Hutchinson Ltd. for 'The Father Christmas on the cake'
from *A moment in rhyme* by Colin West; for 'Freddy' from *Not to
be taken seriously* by Colin West; for 'Toboggan' from *It's funny
when you look at it* by Colin West.
Chatto and Windus, the Hogarth Press, for 'Winter birds' from
Mountains, Polecats and Pheasants by Leslie Norris.
William Collins Sons and Co Ltd. for 'The wicked singers', 'Ghosts'
and 'The frozen man' from *Rabbiting On* by Kit Wright; for
'Christmas Thank You's' from *Swings and Roundabouts* by Mick
Gowar.
Stanley Cook for 'The winter dragon' (from *A fourth poetry book*
edited by John Foster for Oxford University Press), and 'The

holly tree'.

John Cotton for 'A week to Christmas' and 'Riddle'.

J.M. Dent and Sons Ltd. for 'When all the world is full of snow' from *Hurry, hurry Mary dear* by N.M. Bodecker.

André Deutsch Ltd. for 'From the winter wind' from *Mind your own business* by Michael Rosen.

Anne English for 'White December', 'Footsteps in the snow', and 'A change in the weather'.

Faber and Faber Ltd. for 'Snow on snow' from *Season songs* by Ted Hughes.

John Fairfax for 'Christmas Alphabet'.

Eric Finney for 'Pictures on the lawn' and 'Our Nativity play'.

Roy Fuller for 'After breakfast' from *Seen Grandpa lately?* by Roy Fuller (André Deutsch).

David Higham Associates Ltd. for 'At nine of the night I opened my door' from *Figgie Hobbin* by Charles Causley (Macmillan); for 'Christmas stocking' from *The children's bells* by Eleanor Farjeon (Oxford University Press); for 'In the week when Christmas comes' and 'The children's carol' from *Silver sand and snow* by Eleanor Farjeon (Michael Joseph); for 'Kings came riding' by Charles Williams (Oxford University Press); for 'Innocent's song' from *The poems* by Charles Causley (Macmillan); for 'Winter morning' from *An English year* by Clive Sansom (Chatto and Windus); for 'Small, smaller' from *The pedalling man* by Russell Hoban (Worlds Work).

Olwyn Hughes for 'Amulet' from *Moon bells and other poems* by Ted Hughes (Chatto and Windus).

Roderick Hunt for 'Christmas presents' by Eric James, published in *The Oxford Christmas Book for Children* edited by Roderick Hunt, 1981 (Oxford University Press).

Peter Thabit Jones for 'Christmas morning', 'Unable to sleep', 'Castle Gardens, Swansea: Christmas Eve', and 'One shepherd'.

Michael Joseph Ltd. for 'The turkey' from *Animal Alphabet* by Richard Digance.

Peter Little for 'Oh no you don't! Oh yes we do!'

Macmillan Publishing Co. (New York) for 'Bring on the clowns' from *Circus* by Jack Prelutsky.

Brian Moses for 'Christmas Day'.

Judith Nicholls for 'Christmas morning'.

Penguin Books Ltd. for 'Spill' from *Flashlight and other poems* by Judith Thurman (Kestrel Books, 1976); for 'Winter days' from *Salford Road* by Gareth Owen (Kestrel Books).

A.D. Peters and Co. Ltd. for 'The snowman' from *Sky in the pie* by Roger McGough (Kestrel Books).

Putnam Publishing Group (New York) for 'The barn' from *Compass Rose* by Elizabeth Coatsworth (Coward-McCann Inc. — copyright 1929, renewed 1957 by Elizabeth Coatsworth).

John Rice for 'A gift from the stars'.

Robson Books Ltd. for 'Cousin Bert' from *Smile, please* by Shelagh McGee; for 'The shepherds' song' and 'High in the heaven' from *The gift of a lamb* by Charles Causley.

Vernon Scannell for 'The magic show'.

The Society of Authors on behalf of Mrs Iris Wise for 'White Fields' by James Stephens.

Vera Wyse for 'Snow at school'.

Every effort has been made to trace the owners of copyright but we take this opportunity of tendering apologies to any owners whose rights have been unwittingly infringed.

IS A CATERPILLAR TICKLISH?

ed. Adrian Rumble

Here is the ideal poetry anthology for all younger readers, with plenty of colourful and different poems to choose from. There are poems about blackbirds and bulldozers, dragons and dreams, turtles and tomato ketchup, and even about what someone said when he was spanked on the day before his birthday! And with nearly two hundred poems from poets all round the world, there is something here for everyone.

WHEN I DANCE

James Berry

These marvellous poems are directed at young people from all cultures and ethnic backgrounds; they combine life in its exuberance and also its pain, with material drawn from the inner cities of Great Britain and also from the Caribbean.

POETRY JUMP-UP

ed. Grace Nichols

Dynamic, diverse, filled with life and music, here is a collection which brings together the voices of black writers from Britain, Africa, America and Asia and the Caribbean in an exhilarating contemporary anthology, compiled by one of today's top black British writers.

MR BIDERY'S SPIDERY GARDEN
David McCord

There are lots of interesting creatures hiding in this delightful collection of verse for younger children. Everything
from snails and grasshoppers to waltzing mice and coolibahs
are just waiting to be discovered amongst the grass and
leaves of Mr Bidery's spidery garden. With plenty of fun,
rhythm and rhyme, this is a book no one will be able to resist.

NAILING THE SHADOW
Roger McGough

Here is a book for everyone who loves to play with words
and ideas. Stylish and entertaining, it is an unbeatable book
by one of our top poets.

WHISPERS FROM A WARDROBE
Richard Edwards

Wonderful and exciting things happen in Richard Edwards'
book of poems for younger readers. Cushions and coat
hangers talk, and Nittles and Bubberlinks make friends.
And did you know that there are people who breathe
through one ear and people with back to front knees? Enter
a world where nothing is impossible and the incredible is
always true.

AN IMAGINARY MENAGERIE
Roger McGough

From the harmless little bushbaby leading a very dull existence under the stairs to a terrifying man-eating canary, the Imaginary Menagerie is full of unusual and hugely entertaining creatures. The wit and wickedly inventive imagination of Roger McGough combined with Tony Blundell's brilliant drawings will delight both older children and adults alike.

EVERY POEM TELLS A STORY
ed. Raymond Wilson

The perfect book for everyone who likes a good poem and a good story. There are stories to make you laugh and cry and stories to freeze your blood and send shivers down your spine in this collection of compelling stories in verse.

THIRD TIME LUCKY
Mick Gowar

Mick Gowar has a way with words – and poems. He knows what the worst and best things are about school, older sisters, mums, dads – and cats. He can throw you a riddle and cast you a spell, and recreate the special world of daydreams. Jump right in and enjoy yourself!